MUDMASTER: A Program for Calculating Crystalline Size Distributions and Strain from the Shapes of X-Ray Diffraction Peaks: USGS Open-File Report 96-171

et al., D. D. Eberl, V. A. Drits

The BiblioGov Project is an effort to expand awareness of the public documents and records of the U.S. Government via print publications. In broadening the public understanding of government and its work, an enlightened democracy can grow and prosper. Ranging from historic Congressional Bills to the most recent Budget of the United States Government, the BiblioGov Project spans a wealth of government information. These works are now made available through an environmentally friendly, print-on-demand basis, using only what is necessary to meet the required demands of an interested public. We invite you to learn of the records of the U.S. Government, heightening the knowledge and debate that can lead from such publications.

Included are the following Collections:

Budget of The United States Government
Presidential Documents
United States Code
Education Reports from ERIC
GAO Reports
History of Bills
House Rules and Manual
Public and Private Laws
Code of Federal Regulations
Congressional Documents
Economic Indicators
Federal Register
Government Manuals
House Journal
Privacy act Issuances
Statutes at Large

MUDMASTER: A PROGRAM FOR CALCULATING CRYSTALLITE SIZE DISTRIBUTIONS AND STRAIN FROM THE SHAPES OF X-RAY DIFFRACTION PEAKS

By D. D. Eberl[1], V. A. Drits[2], J. Srodon[3] and R. Nüesch[4]

[1]U.S. Geological Survey, 3215 Marine St., Boulder, CO 80303-1066 USA;

[2]Institute of Geology RAN. Pyzevskij 7, 109017 Moscow, Russia;

[3]Institute of Geological Sciences PAN, Senacka 1, 31002 Krakow, Poland;

[4]ETH, Zurich 8092, Switzerland.

U.S. Geological Survey

Open-File Report 96-171

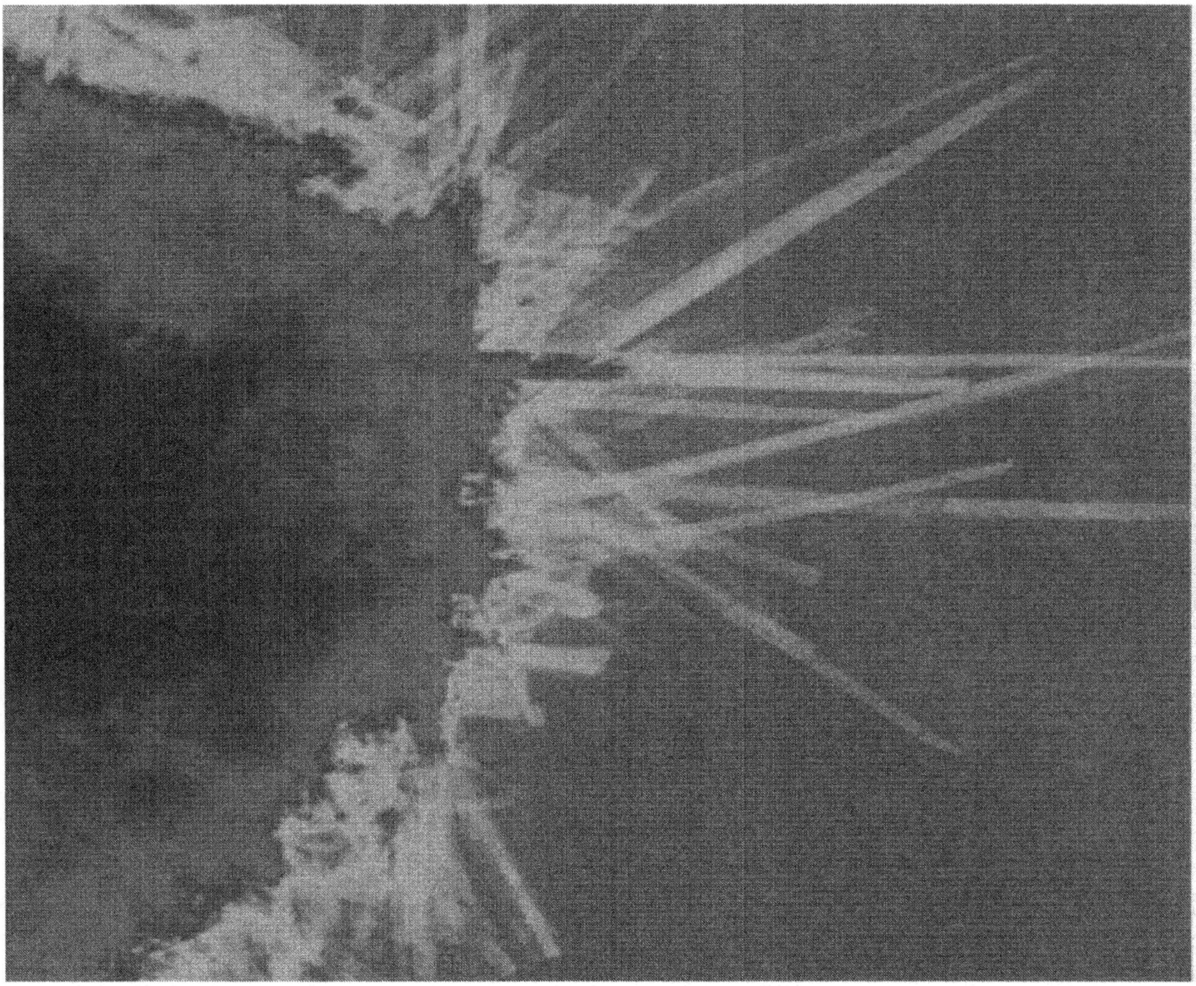

U.S. DEPARTMENT OF THE INTERIOR

BRUCE BABBITT, Secretary

U.S. GEOLOGICAL SURVEY

Gordon Eaton, Director

Last revised: August 16, 2000

Cover photo: Pseudo-color transmission electron micrograph of fibrous, lath-shaped, diagenetic illite (<0.1 μm size fraction) from the Repetto Formation, Santa Barbara Channel, California. Photo by Reed Glasmann.

For additional information and a copy of the program, write or e-mail:

Dennis D. Eberl
U.S. Geological Survey
3215 Marine Street
Boulder, Colorado 80303-1066
USA

ddeberl@usgs.gov

CONTENTS

MUD MASTER

The muddy rivers of spring
Are snarling
Under muddy skies.
The mind is muddy.

As yet, for the mind, new banks
Of bulging green
Are not;
Sky-sides of gold
Are not.
The mind snarls.

....
There is a master of mud.
The shaft of light
Falling, far off, from sky to land,
That is he--

The peach-bud maker,
The mud master,
The master of the mind.

Wallace Stevens

MUDMASTER: A PROGRAM FOR CALCULATING CRYSTALLITE SIZE DISTRIBUTIONS AND STRAIN FROM THE SHAPES OF X-RAY DIFFRACTION PEAKS

D. D. Eberl, V. Drits, J. Írodo~, and R. Nüesch

INTRODUCTION

Particle size may strongly influence the physical and chemical properties of a substance (e.g. its rheology, surface area, cation exchange capacity, solubility, etc.), and its measurement in rocks may yield geological information about ancient environments (sediment provenance, degree of metamorphism, degree of weathering, current directions, distance to shore, etc.). Therefore mineralogists, geologists, chemists, soil scientists, and others who deal with clay-size material would like to have a convenient method for measuring particle size distributions.

Nano-size crystals generally are too fine to be measured by light microscopy. Laser scattering methods give only average particle sizes; therefore particle size can not be measured in a particular crystallographic direction. Also, the particles measured by laser techniques may be composed of several different minerals, and may be agglomerations of individual crystals. Measurement by electron and atomic force microscopy is tedious, expensive, and time consuming. It is difficult to measure more than a few hundred particles per sample by these methods. This many measurements, often taking several days of intensive effort, may yield an accurate mean size for a sample, but may be too few to determine an accurate distribution of sizes.

Measurement of size distributions by X-ray diffraction (XRD) solves these shortcomings. An X-ray scan of a sample occurs automatically, taking a few minutes to a few hours. The resulting XRD peaks average diffraction effects from billions of individual nano-size crystals. The size that is measured by XRD may be related to the size of the individual crystals of the mineral in the sample, rather than to the size of particles formed from the agglomeration of these crystals. Therefore one can determine the size of a particular mineral in a mixture of minerals, and the sizes in a particular crystallographic direction of that mineral.

A shortcoming of the XRD technique is that the size that is measured is the X-ray scattering domain size (crystallite size), which may or may not be equal to crystal size. Therefore, it is important to check the XRD measurements by another method. Comparisons between crystallite thicknesses measured by XRD and crystal thicknesses measured by other methods indicate that these values are the same for fundamental illite crystals (Eberl et al., 1998).

The XRD method is based on the observation that XRD peaks are broadened regularly as a function of decreasing crystallite size. This effect permits accurate measurement of mean crystallite sizes for periodic crystals that range from about 2 nm to about 100 nm. The upper limit for size determination depends significantly on the accuracy of instrumental standards. Reflections for non-periodic systems (for example, basal reflections of irregular mixed-layer structures as well as hkl reflections of minerals containing stacking faults) can not be analyzed by this approach. The crystallite size is equal to $(N-1)d_{(hkl)}$, where N is the number of hkl planes responsible for a reflection. This expression takes into account the fact that layers and planes are not the same, because layers have a thickness. For example, the analysis of kaolinite 00ℓ peaks will give crystallite dimensions perpendicular to the ab plane of the unit cell. If the mean number of diffracting planes is 10, then the number of layer spacings is 9, and the mean thickness is 9 x 7.2 = 64.8 . The term "strain" refers to small fluctuations in the d-spacing of the substance. These d-spacings may be distributed symmetrically or asymmetrically about the substance's mean d-spacing, which corresponds to symmetrical and asymmetrical strain.

This instruction manual covers how to use the program. The theory for its operation is described by Drits et al. (1998), and is based on the previous work of Bertaut (1950) and Warren and Averbach (1950) that was applied to diffraction by metals. The program is available by FTP (see Appendix 5), from ddeberl@usgs.gov, or by writing D. D. Eberl, U.S. Geological Survey, 3215 Marine Street, Boulder, Colorado, USA, 80303-1066.

SYSTEM REQUIREMENTS AND DISCLAIMER

MudMaster will run under either IBM[1] or Macintosh systems. Use of MudMaster requires Microsoft Excel, version 5.0 or greater (the program also is available in version 4.0), and an elementary knowledge of how to use the Excel program (pasting data, changing the axis on a chart, etc.). MudMaster works best on a computer having 16 megabytes or more of RAM. Ten or more megabytes should be assigned to run the Excel program if your system offers an option to assign memory to a program. The program occupies about 5.2 Mb of disk space.

Although this program has been used by the USGS, no warranty, expressed or implied, is made by the USGS or the United States Government as to the accuracy and functioning of the program and related program material nor shall the fact of distribution constitute any such warranty, and no responsibility is assumed by the USGS in connection herewith.

STRUCTURE OF MUDMASTER

The workbook MudMaster is composed of a macrosheet (1-mm.xls) linked to one worksheet (2-mm.xls). In addition, the macrosheet PeakPicker (pp.xls) also is linked to 1-mm.xls. These sheets perform the following functions:

PeakPicker. This macrosheet accepts pasted XRD intensity data as a function of two-theta angle. It is used to inspect the X-ray pattern, to choose the peak to be analyzed, and to calculate an approximate mean thickness for the crystallites by an integral peak width method. The XRD peak may be chosen over a two-theta range that is either symmetrical with respect to the peak maximum, or over any two-theta range that is specified. After the XRD peak has been chosen, PeakPicker automatically can transfer the chosen XRD intensity data into MudMaster and start the MudMaster program.

---

[1] The use of trade, product, industry, or firm names is for descriptive purposes only and does not imply endorsement by the U.S. Government

1-mm.xls (hereafter "sheet 1"). This macrosheet processes the XRD intensities of the peak to be analyzed. These intensities can be pasted directly into this sheet, or can be transferred automatically from PeakPicker. Sheet 1 corrects the XRD peak intensity distribution for the Lorentz-polarization factor (Lp) and layer scattering intensity (G^2) and removes the background, leaving the interference function, which contains information concerning crystallite size distributions and strain. Because experimental data will contain the $K_{\alpha 1}$-$K_{\alpha 2}$ doublet, the program also can remove the $K_{\alpha 2}$ component to the peak if this option is chosen. The interference function 00ℓ maximum, plotted as a function of $2\mathrm{Sin}\theta/\lambda$, then is decomposed into a Fourier series. The Fourier coefficients [A(n) and B(n)] then can be corrected for instrumental broadening (if standards have been introduced into the program - see below) and analyzed for strain, if these options are chosen. Then the corrected Fourier coefficients are pasted into sheet 2, where they are analyzed further for crystallite size and strain.

2-mm.xls (hereafter "sheet 2"). This worksheet uses Fourier coefficients calculated in sheet 1 to perform a Bertaut-Warren-Averbach-type analysis to calculate the mean crystallite size, the crystallite size distribution, the root mean square of the strain, and the strain distributions for the sample. The final results of this analysis are displayed on this sheet, together with other useful data. The crystallite size and strain distributions may be smoothed and truncated to eliminate noise, and the mean size and the size distribution may be corrected for instrumental broadening and for symmetrical strain (if this option was chosen on sheet one).

INSTALLATION OF MUDMASTER

To install the program, copy MudMaster and Samples onto your hard disk, and then open them. The copy must have the name of the original (i.e. MudMastr) to run properly. If the files are compressed, both the Mac version of the program (compressed with the ".sea" extension) and the IBM version (compressed with the ".zip" extension) will decompress automatically when opened. Do not change the name of the program.

The correct LpG^2's for the mineral and, if necessary, for the mineral edges (see below) now are entered automatically into columns K and L in sheet 1 prior to analysis, a change from previous versions of the program which required manual entering. If one uses one's own LpG^2's (e.g. using the "Other" option in sheet 1, cell A23), these LpG^2's must have the same two-theta step size as the XRD peak to be analyzed, should start at two degrees two-theta, and should be entered into columns DP and DQ in sheet 1. LpG^2's other than those contained in the program can be calculated for 2:1 and 2:1:1 clay minerals using the accompanying spreadsheet CALCLPG2. LpG^2's for 1:1 clays can be calculated using Reynolds's NEWMOD program (Reynolds, 1985) by calculating an XRD pattern for a single layer.

Eventually one may want to analyze an instrumental standard, and enter the Fourier coefficients for the standard's XRD peaks into sheet 1, as is discussed below. The current version of the program contains instrumental standards that can be used with our experimental setup (Siemens D500 diffractometer, diffracted beam Söller slits, 1° divergence and 0.15 receiving slits, graphite monochromator, 40 kv and 30 ma tube current). These standards are left in the program as an example, but may not be correct for your experimental setup, and really do not work very well even using our setup. Luckily, with our experimental system, machine broadening does not appear to be a problem, for example, for illites that are 30 nm or less in mean thickness.

DATA REQUIRED

The XRD data should be of high quality (use long count times, a monochromator, a stable generator, excellent equipment adjustment, properly prepared specimen, etc.) and, generally, should be collected in steps of 0.02° two-theta, although any step size can be accommodated by entering the correct LpG^2's into columns DP and DQ, sheet 1, as is discussed above. The program picks the XRD peak position from the peak's maximum intensity; therefore, a peak with a noisy top may be picked in the wrong position. Data should be entered as increasing angles of two-theta. The program can analyze an XRD peak that has 750 analytical points (e.g. a peak that is 15° two-theta broad, having 0.02° steps), and can accept an XRD pattern that contains 2900 analytical points (e.g. 2° to 60° two-theta with 0.02° steps).

EXAMPLES

Example 1: A Simple Analysis

Sample inputs are summarized in Appendix 1, Tables 1-3. Example 1 is the simplest example of how to analyze a sample. The intensities to be analyzed were calculated using the NEWMOD program (Reynolds, 1985) for an 003 reflection for an illite having a lognormal crystallite thickness distribution and a mean crystallite thickness of 10 nm. The peak was calculated for Cu K-alpha radiation only (i.e. no $K_{\alpha1}$- $K_{\alpha2}$ doublet), and does not contain instrumental broadening. The steps for analysis are:

1. Copy the data for sample "LOGNOR, 10" from the "Samples" sheet. This is done by clicking the heading for this column (column B) and by choosing the "Copy" command under the Edit menu. These intensities have been calculated for the 003 illite reflection for a two-theta range of 23.5° to 30.1°, for illite crystallites having a lognormal distribution.
2. Paste this data into column C on sheet 1 by clicking the column heading "C" on sheet 1, and then by choosing the "Paste" command under the Edit menu. The actual data should begin in cell C2. Pasting the entire column automatically clears old data in column C. One can move from PeakPicker to sheet 1 to sheet 2 by clicking the tabs in the lower left corner of the screen.
3. Fill out the "INPUT PARAMETERS" in columns A and B as follows:

Sample name: **Lognormal 10** Input this name in cell A3.

Starting two-theta: **23.5** Input this number in cell A5. It is the starting two-theta angle for the peak to be analyzed which in this case is the same as the starting two-theta for the XRD pattern.

Ending two-theta: **30.1** Input this number in cell A7. This number is the ending two-theta angle for the peak to be analyzed. If the ending two-theta is chosen beyond the end of the intensity data set, the program will not run. The intensity data should contain no zeros.

Step: **0.02** Input this number in cell A9. This value must match the step size of the LpG^2's that are contained in the program (0.02 ° two-theta; these LpG^2's are located in columns DE:DO, sheet 1) or have the same step size as LpG^2's (which must start at 2° two-theta) that the user has entered into columns DP and DQ.

Increment in n for Fourier analysis: **0** Input this number in cell A11. Entering zero will automatically choose an increment in n that is appropriate for the maximum size entered in cell A13, given the space limitations in the program.

Calculate what maximum thickness for the crystallites? **50** Input this number in cell A13. Normally a thickness at least 5 times the mean thickness should be entered here. This value is used to calculate the maximum n to be used in the Fourier analysis for the crystallite size distribution. Using a small thickness saves calculation time, generally does not affect the calculated mean thickness, but may truncate the thickness distribution if the entered value is too small.

Reflection order: **3** Input this number in cell A15. The XRD reflection to be analyzed is the illite 003.

Mineral: **3** Input this number in cell A21. For example, "3" is the index number for illite patterns that have been calculated using Reynolds' NEWMOD computer program. MudMaster uses this input together with the reflection order (entered above) to decide which LpG^2's to use, and which way to flip the peak when the "Autoflip" option is employed (see below).

Expandability (%): **0** Input this number in cell A23. This is the expandability of illite/smectite measured from XRD peak positions of a glycol-solvated sample prior to K-saturation and dehydration. The input is used to calculate the proportion of crystal edges. Because the calculated pattern is simply illite, a zero is entered.

Wavelength detector sees (Å): **1.5418** Input this number in cell A25 for Cu K_α radiation. If the experimental setup includes a monchromator that removes $K_{\alpha 2}$ radiation, then input the value for $K_{\alpha 1}$ here.

Wavelength K-alpha 1 (Å): **1.54051** Input this number in cell A27 for Cu $K_{\alpha 1}$ radiation.

Wavelength K-alpha 2 (Å): **1.54433** Input this number in cell A29 for Cu $K_{\alpha 2}$ radiation.

K-alpha 2/K-alpha 1 intensity ratio?: **0.5** This ratio, normally 0.5, is input in cell A31. It is used in $K_{\alpha 2}$ removal, and will be inactive in the present calculation.

Correct intensities for LpG^2? **2** Input this number in cell B6. If zero is entered, no LpG^2 correction is made; 1 = correction is made only for the interiors of the crystals; 2 = correction is made automatically for the interiors and, if necessary, for the edges of the crystals; 3 = correction is made only for the edges of illite-type crystals (this option generally is not used).

Calculate symmetrical strain? **0** Input this number in cell B8. It is possible to calculate symmetrical strain only if two or more reflections are analyzed. Use of this option will be discussed in a following section.

Remove $K_{\alpha 2}$ radiation? **0** Input this number in cell B10. The NEWMOD patterns are calculated using the K_α wavelength; therefore, there is no need to remove a $K_{\alpha 2}$ component. Removing the $K_{\alpha 2}$ component slows the calculation. Normally, it is adequate to use K_α radiation for clays if the mean crystallite size is less than about 30 nm, and if the two-theta for the peak is less than about 50°.

Do the flip? (0 = no; 1 = left to right; 2 = right to left; 3 = autoflip): **3** Input this number in cell B13. With this option one can restrict analysis to half of the interference function if the other half is disturbed. Theoretically, the interference function is symmetrical; therefore, the other half is generated by rotating half of the function around a vertical axis passing through the interference function's maximum intensity. The rotation can be either from left to right (enter "1") or from right to left (enter "2"). If a "3" is entered, the program automatically will choose the correct flip direction for the clay to be analyzed, according to Table 4 in

Appendix 2. The flipping option may be used if the mineral's layer scattering intensity is equal to zero (or extremely small) in the vicinity of the XRD peak, or if XRD intensities from other minerals obscure half of the peak. The flip option will be discussed further in Example 2 below.

Iterate for proportion of edges? **1** Input this number in cell B15. Entering a "1" will cause the program to iterate until the proportion of edges used in the calculation of LpG^2 is appropriate for the mean size given in cell H3, sheet 2. This iteration generally is performed only for the illite 001 reflection, hence a "2" is normally used here.

Other information: **NEWMOD calculated pattern** Input this information in cell B17.

Update screen? **0** Input this number in cell B19. Calculation is faster if the screen is not updated. The screen automatically will update at the end of the calculations. Input a number other than zero to watch the program make the calculations.

4. Click the button labeled, "Start MudMaster."
5. The results will appear on sheet 2 in about 10 seconds when using a Power Macintosh G3 computer. The results can be printed by choosing "Print" in the file menu. The results are as follows:

Sample name: The sample name, **Lognormal 10**, appears in cell A2. The mineral chosen for analysis, **NEWMOD CALC. ILLITE**, is given in cell H1.

Best mean (nm; extrapolated): **10.0** This area-weighted, mean crystallite size is calculated, according to the theory of Warren and Averbach (1950), by extrapolation of the steepest slope of a plot of the corrected Fourier coefficients [H(S)] versus S to an H(S) of zero (see plot labeled "Extrapolated Mean" in sheet 2). The extrapolated mean is said to be the "best mean" because it is unaffected by smoothing or by ripples that sometimes affect the mean calculated from the distribution, and also because it is unaffected by the maximum thickness entered in cell A13 on sheet 1.

Mean (nm; distribution): **10.0** This mean is calculated from the distribution that is shown in the chart labeled, "Thickness (Area-weighted frequency)." It should equal the "best mean."

Its value may change if one changes the smoothing power or the distribution limit (see below). The solid curve given in the distribution figure is for a theoretical lognormal curve that has been calculated from the measured distribution.

Alpha (from nm): **2.16** This parameter, which is mean of the natural logarithms of the crystallite sizes, is calculated from the distribution.

Beta^2: **0.29** This parameter, which is the variance of the natural logarithms of the crystallite sizes, is calculated from the distribution.

Volume-weighted mean (nm): **13.2** This volume weighted mean is calculated from the distribution (see Appendix 4).

Position interference function (two-theta): **26.80** This value corresponds to the position of the peak intensity of the interference function 003 maximum.

d-spacing (Å): **3.327** This value corresponds to the 003 maximum of the interference function.

Root mean square strain (Å): **Not calculated** The strain calculation requires at least two peaks for analysis, and therefore was not calculated. It will be discussed in more detail below.

Approximate fundamental particle thickness (nm): **10.0** This value is calculated from the approximate mean thickness and expandability entered on sheet 1 according to an equation given by Drits et al. (1998). If the expandability entered into sheet 1 is greater than zero, then this value refers to the mean thickness of fundamental illite particles found in mixed-layer illite/smectite. Otherwise this value is the same as the approximate mean thickness entered into sheet 1.

Illite fixed cations/ half-unit cell **Not applicable** This value is calculated only for PVP-illites by assuming a fixed cation content of 0.89 equivalents per $O_{10}(OH)_2$ for illite layers.

Specific a-b surface area **74** This value is calculated from the clay mineral density (2.7 g/cm^3) that is found in cell L16

Hidden knobs set at recommendation?: **Yes** A "yes" indicates that all of the recommended settings are used on sheet 1, cells E7 to E33. These hidden knobs and switches are used in program development, and normally should not be changed.

Cells H27:H56: These cells repeat the values entered on sheet 1.

6. One can input parameters on sheet 2 to refine the results of the calculations for the crystallite size distribution and the strain:

Dist. Limit? (nm): Input **50** in B2. This option can be used to truncate the distribution at a chosen crystallite size. It is used to eliminate ripples and noise at large sizes in the distribution. If the distribution is disturbed by such noise, the distribution limit can be adjusted so as to reduce the difference between the distribution mean given in cell H5 and the extrapolated mean given in cell H3.

Smooth power: Input **1** in B4. This option smoothes the crystallite size, strain and volume distributions. The larger the number entered, the greater the smoothing. A small smoothing power (e.g. 0 to 1) is best, because large smoothing powers will distort the distributions. The distributions are smoothed by using a moving average that is centered on the number to be smoothed. A smoothing power of 1 includes one number on either side of the number to be smoothed, and therefore averages 3 numbers; a smoothing power of 2 includes two numbers on either side, and therefore averages 5 numbers to calculate the smoothed number; etc. Both the first and second derivatives of the Fourier coefficients are smoothed in this manner.

Symmetrical strain correction?: **Input 0** in D2. If a "**1**" is entered here, and if at least two XRD peaks related by n in Bragg's law (e.g. the 001 and the 002; or the 114 and the 228) have been analyzed for a sample under the strain option (cell B8 in sheet 1), the means given in cells H3 and H5, and the distributions given in the charts are corrected for the effects of symmetrical strain. Prior to correction, symmetrical strain causes reflections to give progressively smaller mean crystallite sizes with increasing reflection order. The strain calculation is discussed in more detail in Example 3, below.

Instrumental correction?: Input **0** in D4. If a "**1**" is entered here, the mean size and distributions are corrected for instrumental broadening, provided instrumental standards have been entered into columns CS to DB in sheet 1 (see below). A zero is entered here for this analysis because NEWMOD calculated patterns do not contain machine broadening. Normally, correction for instrumental broadening is not needed if the mean crystallite size is less than about 30 nm. Correction for instrumental broadening may distort distributions. This procedure has not been refined fully.

8. The results can now be printed by pushing the printer button on the Tools Bar, or by choosing "Print..." in the File menu.

Example 2: Using PeakPicker and doing the flip

The following steps indicate how to use PeakPicker in an analysis of the kaolinite 001 reflection.

1. Clear column E in macro sheet pp.xls, and then copy the data for sample GA KAOLINITE from the "Samples" sheet, and paste it into column E in PeakPicker. The first data point should be entered into cell E2, and the sample name should be in cell E1.
2. Fill in the "INPUT" in columns B and C in pp.xls as follows:

Step size (deg. two-theta): **0.02** Input this number in cell B4. This value is the two-theta angle step size at which the data was collected. It normally is 0.02° two-theta.

Update screen?: **0** Input this number in cell B6. Entering zero yields the faster calculation time. Enter "1" to watch the calculation take place.

Plot pattern? (1 = yes): **1** Input this number in cell B8. With this option set to "1", the intensity data that was input in column E will be plotted as a function of two-theta angle in a chart to be labeled with the sample's name.

Pick symmetrical peak? (1 = yes): **1** Input this number in cell B10. Normally a zero is entered here, but we are taking a small digression to demonstrate how to calculate an approximate mean size. If "**1**" is chosen, the program automatically will pick a peak that is symmetrical in two-theta with respect to the peak maximum. In other words, the number of degrees two-theta between the left side of the peak (to be entered as the exact starting angle in cell C8) and the peak maximum will be used for the right side of the peak. If this cell is not set equal to one, the two-theta range for the peak will be chosen between the angles entered into the exact starting angle (cell C8) and the ending angle (cell C10). For either option, if the ending two-theta is chosen beyond the end of the intensity data set, the program will not run.

Sample length correction? **0** Input this number in cell B12. At low two-theta angles some of the X-ray beam may miss the sample. The importance of this effect depends on the goniometer radius, the angle of the divergence slit, and the sample length. To use this option, enter these values for your experimental setup in cells G5, G7 and G9.

Calculate approximate mean? **3** Input this number in cell B16. Normally a zero is entered here because calculation of an approximate mean is unnecessary for Fourier analysis of the pattern by MudMaster; but an example of how to use this option is given here in this brief digression. A "1" is entered to calculate an approximate thickness by the integral peak width method of Drits et al. (1997; developed for illite); "2" and "3" assume an asymptotic or a lognormal shape to the distribution, respectively, and use equations relating integral peak width and thickness given in Figure 8 in Eberl et al. (1998). These equations, developed for illite fundamental particle thicknesses, frequently work for other clays and minerals. Option 4 is an empirical relation found for PVP-intercalated illiltes.

d 001 (Å): **7.2** Input this number in cell B18. This input is used to calculate the approximate thickness using an integral peak width method.

Sample name: GA Kaolinite Do not enter anything in cell C4. The sample name automatically will be entered here from the top of column E when the program is started.

Starting angle for all intensities: **2** Input this number in cell C6. The XRD pattern for this kaolinite starts at 2° two-theta.

Exact starting angle for analysis: **6** Input this number in cell C8. This two-theta angle is the left side of the peak to be analyzed. See Table 4 in Appendix 2 for the recommended settings for kaolinite, or see the chart in pp.xls by scrolling down.

End angle for analysis: **13** Input this number in cell C10. This two-theta angle approximately marks the right side of the peak to be analyzed.

Reflection order: **1** Input this number in cell C12. We are analyzing the kaolinite 001 reflection.

Calculate strain?: **0** Input this number in cell C14. The strain option will be discussed below.

Autopaste?: **0** Input this number in cell C17. Set it to zero to do calculations in PeakPicker only. Enter "1" to paste results from the PeakPicker calculation into sheet 1. Enter "2" to paste results into sheet 1 and to start the MudMaster program.

3. Click the button "Start PeakPicker." The XRD pattern will be plotted in the chart labeled with the sample's name. The kaolinite 001 reflection can be examined more closely by enlarging the chart (pull out the corner of the chart) and changing its scale (double click on the values next to the x- and y-axes). An approximate mean of 22.1 nm appears in cell A13. This is the end of the description concerning how to calculate an approximate mean, and the beginning of the exact analysis. Set cell B8 to **0** (because the pattern already has been plotted), cell B10 to **0** (to avoid the minimum in LpG^2 when calculating the interference function), cell B14 to zero (no need to calculate the approximate mean again), and cell C17 to **1**, so that the X-ray data will be transferred to 1-mm.xls. Start the program again.
4. The intensity data now has been processed, and pasted into 1-mm.xls. Now fill in the appropriate input options on sheet 1 as follows:

Sample name: **GA Kaolinite** (Filled in automatically from PeakPicker.)

Starting two-theta: **6.00** (Filled in automatically from PeakPicker.)

Ending two-theta: **13.00** (Filled in automatically from PeakPicker.)

Step size: **0.02** (Filled in automatically from PeakPicker.)

Increment in n for Fourier analysis: **0**

Calculate what maximum thickness for the crystallites?: **100**

Reflection order: **1** (Filled in automatically from PeakPicker.)

Mineral: **10**

Expandability: **0**

Wavelength detector sees (Å): **1.5418**

Wavelength K-alpha 1 (Å): **1.54051**

Wavelength K-alpha 2 (Å): **1.54433**

K-alpha 2/K-alpha 1 intensity ratio?: **0.5**

Correct for LpG^2?: **2** Inputting "2" will have the program automatically choose the appropriate LpG^2 correction for this mineral (kaolinite) and this reflection (the 001). Because only the interior LpG^2 is used for the kaolinite calculation (see recommendations in Table 4), one also could enter a "1" here.

Calc. symm. strain?: **0** (Filled in automatically from PeakPicker.)

Remove K-alpha 2 radiation?: **0** Inputting a "1" in cell B10 will cause the program to separate K_α radiation into its two components by a Fourier technique (Gangulee, 1970), and the $K_{\alpha 1}$ component would be used in subsequent analysis. Inputting a zero will cause the radiation that the detector sees (normally K_α radiation) to be used. Generally, for determining clay thicknesses it is sufficient to use K_α radiation.

Do the flip? **3** If one decides to flip, then one chooses the left half of the kaolinite 001 interference function maximum for analysis, because the layer scattering intensity for the right half approaches zero (Figure 8 in Appendix 3). In Figure 8, the Lorentz-polarization function (Lp) times the layer scattering intensity (G^2) is plotted on top of the kaolinite XRD pattern. The intensity of an XRD peak = $(Lp)(G^2)(\varphi)$, where φ is the interference function, a function which carries the crystallite size and strain information. Division of the XRD data by LpG^2 to find the interference function may lead to an unrealistically large intensity for the right half of the 00ℓ interference function maximum and to an asymmetrical form. Therefore only the left half of the peak can be used. Table 4 and the other figures in Appendix 3 show that the problem also exists for other clay XRD peaks, for example, for the illite 001 and 002 illite reflections. Entering a "1" flips the peak from left to right; entering a "2" flips it from right to left; and entering a "3" automatically flips the peak according to the recommendations given in Table 4 in Appendix 2.

Iterate for proportion of edges? **0** or **2** There is no need to iterate, because crystal edges are not used in the calculation for kaolinite.

Other information: **Well-crystallized CMS source clay; 5 sec/step**

Update screen? **0**

5. Start MudMaster. Using a Power Macintosh G3 computer, the results of the calculation appear in about 12 seconds on sheet 2. The two-theta scale needs to be changed on the appropriate chart (double click on the scale to change it) in order to display the interference function. *One should always check the interference function plot to see if it looks realistic*. The profile of the maximum should be symmetrical, and must have a background that reaches zero on either side of the peak. The calculation gives a best mean of 16.8 nm and a mean for the distribution of 16.8 nm using a distribution limit of 65, a smoothing power of 1, and no correction for instrumental broadening. The thickness distribution shown in the chart (red diamond symbols) is very different from the theoretical lognormal distribution calculated from the same data (black solid curve). One also should always check the chart for the extrapolated mean to be sure that the solid line finds the steepest slope of the plotted data. If the solid line lies above the data, one should extend the range for which the program searches for the steepest slope in cells L4 and L5 in sheet 2. If one enters a smoothing power of zero (cell B4), the distribution appears to have a vibration. This error is related to the presence of a small illite peak in the low-angle tail of the kaolinite reflection (see the kaolinite pattern in PeakPicker, and, if necessary, enlarge the vertical scale). If this illite peak is removed (by using the program PeakChopper) prior to MudMaster analysis, the vibrations, which were dampened previously by using a smoothing power of 1, disappear. It is always better to use a smoothing power of zero, if possible, so as not to distort the shape of the distribution.

Example 3: Symmetrical strain analysis

The following is an example of how to correct the mean crystallite size for symmetrical strain:

1. Copy the data for sample "K-Zemp-H" from the "Samples" sheet, and paste it into column E in PeakPicker. This pattern is of an illite/smectite sample (Zempleni illite/smectite) that has been K-saturated, heated at 300° C overnight to collapse all smectite layers, and then X-rayed in dry air. Prior to dehydration it was 15% expandable.
2. Analyze the pattern in PeakPicker as was described above for kaolinite. Choose a two-theta range and other settings according to the recommendations for illite in Table 4.
3. Enter the settings in sheet 1 as follows:

   Sample name: **K-Zemp-H** (entered automatically from PeakPicker)

   Starting two-theta: **4.4** (entered automatically from PeakPicker)

   Ending two-theta: **9.0** (entered automatically from PeakPicker)

   Step size: **0.02** (entered automatically from PeakPicker)

   Increment in n for Fourier analysis: **0**

   Calculate what max thickness?: **50**

   Reflection order: **1**

   Mineral: **1**

   Expandability (%): **15** (measured for a glycol-solvated sample)

   Wavelength detector sees: **1.5418**

   Wavelength K-alpha 1: **1.54051**

   Wavelength K-alpha 2: **1.54433**

   K-alpha2/K-alpha 1 intensity ratio? **0.5**

   Correct intensities for LpG2? **2**

   Calc. symm. strain? **1** The succession number of the peak in the analysis is entered here (also can be entered from PeakPicker). Entering a "0" or a "1" will erase all previously stored strain data. For the second peak to be analyzed, a "2" should be entered here; for the third a "3"; etc. Note that his number may differ from the reflection order.

Remove K-alpha 2 radiation? **0**

Do the flip? **3**

Iterate for proportion of edges?: **2** Iterate the calculation only for the 001 reflection.

Other information: **K-saturated I/S heated to 300° C overnight**

Update screen during calculation? **0**

5. Push the start button. The results in sheet 2 give an extrapolated mean of 10.7 nm and a lognormally-shaped distribution having a mean of 10.7 nm, using a smoothing power of 0 and a distribution limit of 35.
6. Choose a second peak for analysis that is related to the first peak by "n"' in Bragg's law. For example, analyze the 002 peak in the same manner by running PeakPicker, and by entering the following parameters in sheet 1:

Sample name: **K-Zemp-H** (entered automatically from PeakPicker)

Starting two-theta: **13.20** (entered automatically from PeakPicker)

Ending two-theta: **18.00** (entered automatically from PeakPicker)

Step size: **0.02** (entered automatically from PeakPicker)

Increment in n for Fourier analysis: **1**

Calculate what max thickness? **50**

Reflection order: **2**

Mineral: **1**

Expandability (%): **15**

Wavelength detector sees: **1.5418**

Wavelength K-alpha 1: **1.54051**

Wavelength K-alpha 2: **1.54433**

K-alpha 2/K-alpha 1 intensity ratio?: **0.5**

Correct intensities for LpG2? **2**

Calc symm strain? **2**

Remove K-alpha 2 radiation?: **0**

Do the flip? **3**

Iterate for proportion of edges? **2** In general, iterate only for the smallest order reflection.

Other information: **K-saturated I/S heated to 300° C overnight**

Update screen during calculation? **0**

7. Start the program. The means on sheet 2 now can be corrected for the presence of symmetrical strain by entering "1" in cell D2, but it is better to continue the analysis to include the 005 reflection, analyzed in a similar fashion, to receive a more accurate value for the strain. A quartz reflection is hidden beneath the illite 003 reflection, as can be deduced from the presence of another quartz reflection at 20.84° two-theta; therefore the 003 is not suitable for analysis. After the 005 has been analyzed, the extrapolated mean thickness, not corrected for strain, equals 5.9 nm; corrected for strain the mean equals 11.1 nm. The distribution, plotted using a distribution limit of 26 and a smoothing power of 1, is somewhat distorted because a small XRD peak lies in the low-angle tail of the 005 reflection. It would have been better to flip the 005 peak from right to left, rather than from left to right, as was done under the autoflip option (cell B13, sheet 1). A right to left flip is practical for the 005 illite reflection because LpG^2 does not approach zero on the right side of this peak (see Figure 1). A plot of the root mean square of the symmetrical strain as a function of layer thickness is presented on sheet 2, as are plots of lnA(n) versus ℓ^2, the slopes of which are used to determine the strain. The root mean square of the strain equals 0.371 Å (using a smoothing power of 1) if the region that the program searches for the strain (set in cells L11 and L12, sheet 2) is set at 2 to 12, which includes a plateau in the root mean square strain values (see this chart by scrolling down). If the root mean square of the strain is constant with thickness, as it is in this analysis because there is a plateau in the previously mentioned chart, then the strain has a Gaussian distribution, the positive half of which is graphed in a chart labeled "Strain Distribution" in sheet 2. If there is no such plateau in the root mean square strain, then the Strain Distribution chart is meaningless. Other charts on this page also are corrected for strain if a "1" is entered into

cell D2. The data for this sample listed in Table 3 of Drits et al. (1998) were collected using an earlier version of the program, and have been superseded by the present calculation.

Other examples: MOM, HUMPS, MUM, Mt. Washington, and ZEMP-PVP

The NEWMOD calculated illite XRD patterns labeled MOM and HUMPS in the "Samples" worksheet also can be pasted into 1-mm.xls and analyzed (using Cu K_α radiation) as illite 003 reflections between 23.5 and 30.1° two-theta. The distribution for MOM (use an approximate mean crystallite thickness of 30 nm) should spell out this word, and HUMPS (use an approximate mean crystallite size of 40 nm) should give a distribution containing 14 evenly spaced and equally sized modes between thicknesses of 2 to 200 nm. These two samples can be used to study the effects of smoothing, flipping, etc. on the shapes of the distributions. The data labeled "MUM" (mean = 48.5 nm) and "Mt. Washington" (mean = 6 nm) were calculated from 2 to 50° two-theta using NEWMOD by adding together separately calculated patterns for $K_{\alpha1}$ and $K_{\alpha2}$ radiation in the ratio 2:1. The former distribution should spell the word "MUM", whereas the latter should yield a symmetrical distribution starting at 2 nm, ending at 10 nm, with a maximum at 6 nm. This latter distribution is perhaps more accurately calculated using an LpG^2 corrected for K-content, rather than using pyrophyllite edges, although the edge-type calculation is more convenient to program. These patterns can be used to study the effects of $K_{\alpha2}$ removal, reflection order, flipping, etc. on the mean size and size distribution. Analysis (using 001 reflection) of the PVP-illite sample named ZEMP-PVP gives a mean thickness of 4.8 nm, with a lognormally-shaped distribution having an alpha = 1.48, B^2 = 0.20, and a d-spacing of 9.892 Å. This is the same clay analyzed above as a K-saturated, heated illite/smectite. Analysis of the K-saturated, dehydrated sample gives the thickness of dehydrated MacEwan crystallites (stacks of fundamental illite particles), whereas analysis of the PVP-sample gives the thickness of the fundamental illite particles themselves (Eberl et al., 1998).

STANDARDS

In addition to crystallite size effects and strain, XRD peaks also will be broadened by XRD instrumental effects. These effects are removed by using an instrumental standard (which should be composed of many crystallites) containing effectively infinitely large crystallites that have no strain. Instrumental broadening does not lead to serious errors if the mean crystallite size is small.

Thicker crystals require an instrumental standard, and for this purpose we use the greater than 20 micrometer size fraction of the National Bureau of Standards Standard Reference Material 675, a synthetic fluorophlogopite. This size fraction was prepared by repeated (seven times) settling in water. Then a thin, oriented film was prepared for X-ray diffraction analysis by drying a suspension of the material on a non-diffracting substrate (polished silicon wafer cut perpendicular to the 100 axis). A glass slide is inappropriate as a substrate because it gives an X-ray background which tends to broaden the XRD peaks.

To develop a standard for your instrument, X-ray the standard using exactly the same slit system and step size that you plan to use for crystallite size analysis. Then enter the raw XRD intensities into PeakPicker and MudMaster using $K_{\alpha 1}$ radiation, as is described above. When the MudMaster analysis has finished, copy the values for the Fourier coefficients [A(n) and B(n)], found in columns BK and BL of sheet 1, and paste them into the appropriate columns for the angular range over which the standard peak is to operate (columns CS to DB in sheet 1). Ripples and noise in the distribution for the standard at large sizes can be eliminated by setting A(n) and B(n) for these sizes equal to constants, the constants being the last useful calculated values for A(n) and B(n). Then cell D4 in sheet 2 is set equal to "**1**" to remove the effect of instrumental broadening for a sample.

The approach for using instrumental standards has yet to be resolved satisfactorily. We run most of our analyses without instrumental standards, an approximation which gives satisfactory results up to a mean size of at least 30 nm for illites.

OTHER ANALYSIS HINTS

One needs to include all of the tails of the XRD peaks to be analyzed. Analysis should extend from one half the distance between the peak to be analyzed and the adjacent reflections that are related to it by n in Bragg's law. Failure to include all of the tails may lead to noisy distributions and incorrect means.

The analyzed peak needs to be free from any other factors that might broaden it (i.e. non-periodicity in the analyzed direction of the crystallites) and from the presence of interfering XRD peaks. Analysis of illite and illite/smectite samples is particularly tricky, and one should refer to the papers by Drits et al. (1998) and Eberl et al. (1998).

It may be possible to calculate a good mean size for many samples even if G^2 is not known by using option 13 in cell A23, sheet 1. The LpG^2 function for many clays can be calculated by using the accompanying program CALCLPG2.

The program yields area-weighted mean sizes for X-ray scattering domains. These domains may or may not equal true particle size; therefore, it is wise to verify the XRD measurements by another technique. As was discussed previously, this verification has been made for illite fundamental particle thickness measurements. For these minerals the X-ray scattering domains generally equal fundamental illite particle thicknesses (Eberl et al., 1998).

ACKNOWLEDGMENTS

We thank John Neil and Gene Whitney for reviewing this manuscript and the program.

REFERENCES

Bertaut, F., 1950, Raies de Debye-Scherrer et répartition des dimensions des domaines de Bragg dans les poudres polycristallines: Acta Crystallographica, v. 3, p. 14-18.

Drits, V. A., Írodo~, J., and Eberl, D. D., 1997, XRD measurement of the mean crystallite thickness of illite and illite/smectite: reappraisal of the Kubler index and the Scherrer equation: Clays & Clay Minerals, v. 45, p. 461-475.

Drits, V. A., Eberl, D. D., and Írodo~, J., 1998, XRD measurement of the mean thickness, thickness distribution and strain for illite and illite/smectite crystallites by the Bertaut-Warren-Averbach technique: Clays & Clay Minerals, v. 46, p. 38-50.

Eberl, D. D., Drits, V. A., and Írodo~, J., 1998, Deducing growth mechanisms for minerals from the shapes of crystal size distributions: American Journal of Science, v. 298, p. 499-533.

Eberl, D. D., Nüesch, R., Sucha, V., and Tsipursky, S., 1998, Measurement of the thickness of fundamental illite particles by X-ray diffraction using PVP-10 intercalation: Clays & Clay Minerals, v. 46, p. 89-97.

Eberl, D. D., Írodo~, J., Kralik, M., Taylor, B., and Peterman, Z. E., 1990, Ostwald ripening of clays and metamorphic minerals, Science, v. 248, p. 474-477.

Gangulee, A., 1970, Separation of the $\alpha_1 - \alpha_2$ doublet in X-ray diffraction profiles: Journal of Applied Crystallography, v. 3, p. 272-277.

Klug, H. P. and Alexander, L. E., 1974, *X-ray Diffraction Procedures for Polycrystalline and Amorphous Materials*, second edition, John P. Wiley and Sons, Inc., N.Y., 966 p.

Reynolds, R.C., Jr., 1985, NEWMOD©, a Computer Program for the Calculation of One-Dimensional Diffraction Patterns of Mixed-Layered Clays: R. C. Reynolds, Jr., 8 Brook Dr., Hanover, New Hampshire, 03755.

Warren, B. E., and Averbach, B. L., 1953, The effect of cold-work distortion on X-ray patterns: Journal of Applied Physics, v. 21, p. 595-599.

APPENDIX 1: SUMMARY OF PROGRAM INPUTS

Table 1. Summary of PeakPicker (pp.xls) Inputs.

Input	Cell	Value	Comments
Step size (degrees 2-theta)	B4	2-theta value	Analytical step size (usually 0.02° two-theta).
Update screen?	B6	0 or 1	Input "0" for faster calculation, "1" to watch calculation.
Plot pattern?	B8	1 = yes	Input "1" plots entire XRD pattern in chart labeled with the sample's name.
Pick symm. peak?	B10	1 = yes	"1" picks XRD peak symmetrically with respect to starting angle (C8) and peak maximum; otherwise the peak is picked between angles entered in cells C8 and C10.
Sample length correction?	B12	1 = yes	To use this option, experimental setup must be entered in cells G5, G7 and G9.
Calc approx mean?	B16	0 = no; or 1, 2 or 3.	Calculates an approximate thickness (see cell A13) by various integral peak width methods. 1= DSE method; 2 = assumes asymptotic shape to size distribution; 3 = assumes lognormal shape to size distribution.
d 001 (Å)	B18	10 for illite; 7.2 for kaolinite; etc.	This value is used in the calculation of the approximate crystallite thickness by an integral peak width method (see cell B14).

Sample name	C4	Name of sample	Entered automatically from cell E1.
Start angle for all intensities	C6	2-theta value	2-theta value for start of XRD pattern
Exact start angle for analysis	C8	2-theta value	Exact starting angle (left, low-angle side) of XRD peak to be analyzed. Be sure to include al of peak's tail (see Table 4).
End angle for analysis	C10	2-theta value	Approximate end angle of this peak. C10 must be greater than C8.
Reflection order	C12	Whole number	Order of reflection analyzed.
Calc strain?	C14	0 to 5	0 = no; or give analysis number, up to a maximum of 5.
Autopaste?	C17	0, 1 or 2	"0" stays in pp.xls program; "1' pastes results i 1-mm.xls; "2" pastes and starts 1-mm.xls.

Table 2. Summary of MudMaster Sheet 1 (1-mm.xls) Inputs.

Input	**Cell**	**Value**	**Comments**
Sample name	A3	sample name	Filled in automatically if PeakPicker is used.
Starting two-theta	A5	2-theta value	2-theta for start (left side) of XRD peak to be analyzed; filled in automatically if PeakPicker is used
Ending two-theta	A7	2-theta value	2-theta for end (right side) of XRD peak to be analyzed; filled in automatically if PeakPicker is used.
Step size	A9	degrees 2-theta	Be sure that step size of LpG^2, entered into columns K and L, sheet 1, is the same as this entry. Filled in automatically if PeakPicker is used.
Increment in n for Fourier	A11	whole number	Normally use 0.
Calculate what max thickness?	A13	whole number	Enter the largest thickness to be calculated for the crystallite size distribution (generally 5 times approximate mean thickness).
Reflection order	A17	whole number	Largest common denominator for the indices of the analyzed peak

Mineral	A23	1 through 13	This entry is used to decide which way to flip the interference function if the "Autoflip" option is used in cell B13, and for choosing the correct LpG^2.
Expandability (%)	A25	0 to 100	Enter expandability of mixed-layer illite/smectite prior to K-saturation and dehydration. Set at 0 for illite and other clays.
Wavelength detector sees	A27	in Å-units	Usually K-alpha (for example, Cu $K_\alpha = 1.5418$) unless $K_{\alpha 2}$ has been eliminated by using a monochromator.
Wavelength K-alpha 1	A29	in Å-units	Wavelength to be used in MudMaster analysis. For example, Cu $K_{\alpha 1} = 1.54051$ Å.
Wavelength K-alpha 2	A31	in Å-units	Wavelength to be used in MudMaster analysis. For example, Cu $K_{\alpha 2} = 1.54433$ Å.
K-alpha 2/K-alpha 1 intensity ratio	A33	normally 0.5	Use 0.5, unless you have found a different value using the method of Gangulee (1970).
Correct intensities for LpG^2?	B6	0, 1 or 2	0 = do not correct XRD intensities for LpG^2, 1 = correct only for interiors of crystals; 2 = automatically correct for interiors and, if necessary, for edges of crystals; 3 = correct only

			for edges. LpG2's are stored in columns DE:DQ, sheet 1.
Calculate symm. strain?	B8	0 through 5	"0" turns this option off. Otherwise input the number of the peak in the strain analysis to a maximum of 5 peaks. A "0" or a "1" erases previously stored strain data.
Remove K-alpha 2 radiation?	B10	1 = yes	Generally, K_{α} radiation can be used for clays.
Do the flip?	B13	0, 1, 2 or 3	"0" uses the analytical interference function for subsequent Fourier analysis; "1" takes half this peak and flips it left to right; "2" flips it right to left. "3" automatically flips peak in direction given in Table 4, Appendix 2.
Iterate for proportion of edges?	B15	0 = no; 1 = yes; 2 = only for illite 001 reflection	Iterates calculation until proportion of edges used to calculate LpG2 is appropriate to the mean calculated. Generally used only for illite.
Other information	B17	Information	
Update screen?	B19	1 = yes	Program runs faster if screen is not updated.

Table 3. Summary of MudMaster Sheet 2 (2-mm.xls) Inputs.

Input	**Cell**	**Value**	**Comments**
Distribution Limit?	B2	in nm	Sets the limit to the distribution charts. Used to eliminate ripples and noise at large sizes.
Smooth Power	B4	whole number	Increasing this number increases the degree of smoothing. Best to use a small number (0 to 1)
Strain Correction?	D2	0 = no; 1 = yes	If more than one peak has been analyzed for symmetrical strain (cell B8 in sheet 1), then entering a "1" will apply the strain correction to the means and the distributions. The peaks also will be corrected for instrumental broadening, if cell E11 in sheet 1 is set equal to 1.
Instrument correction?	D4	1 = yes	Inputting "1" will cause the mean and distribution to be corrected for instrumental broadening, if proper standards have been entered in 1-mm.xls. Strain corrected means wi not be corrected for instrumental broadening unless a "1" was entered into cell E11, sheet 1, prior to calculation.

APPENDIX 2: RECOMMENDED SETTINGS FOR CLAY ANALYSES

Table 4. Recommended Settings for Analysis of Clay Basal Reflections

Mineral:	**Reflection Order:**	**Flip**	**2-theta of max:**	**Two-theta Range:**	**Pick symm. peak? (1 = yes):**
Dehyd K-illite**,	001	L to R	8.8°	4.4° to 9.0°	0
PVP-illite*, and	002	L to R	17.7°	13.3° to 18°	0
NEWMOD illite	003***	R to L	26.8°	25° to 31.5^{2}	0
	004	L to R	36.0°	31.5° to 36.4°	0
	005***	L to R	45.3°	40.9° to 46°	0
Kaolinite and	001	L to R	12.3°	6° to 13°	0
serpentine	002	None	24.7°	18° to 26°	0
	003	None	37.5°	31° to 44°	1
2-glycol smectite	001	L to R	5.2°	2° to 9°	0
	002	R to L	10.47°	10° to 13.1°	0
	003	R to L	15.7°	15° to 18.4°	0
	005	R to L	26.4°	26° to 29°	0
2-H_2O smectite	001	L to R	5.9°	2.9° to 6°	0
	003	L to R	17.7°	14.7° to 18°	0
	005	L to R	29.8°	26.8° to 30°	0
1-H_2O smectite	001	L to R	7.1°	3.5° to 8°	0
	002	R to L	14.2°	14° to 17.7°	0
	004	L to R	28.8°	25.2° to 29°	0

Mg-tri-trichlorite	001	L to R	6.2°	3° to 6.5°	0
	002	R to L	12.5°	12° to 15.6°	0
	003	R to L	19°	18° to 22.1°	0
	004	R to L	25.1°	24° to 28.2°	0
	005	L to R	31.5°	28.3° to 32°	0
	007	None	41.4°	42° to 47.8°	1
Pyrophyllite and talc	001	L to R	9.6°	4.5° to 10°	0
	002	L to R	19.3°	14.3° to 20°	0
	003	L to R	29.1°	24° to 30°	0

* See Eberl et al. (1998)

** See Drits et al. (1998).

*** Also can be flipped in opposite direction, or not flipped.

APPENDIX 3: PLOTS OF LpG^2 AND XRD PATTERNS FOR CLAY MINERAL BASAL REFLECTIONS

These patterns are presented so that one can tell whether or not the "Flip" option needs to be used when analyzing a peak. Flipping is needed if LpG^2 approaches zero in the vicinity of the peak to be analyzed. LpG^2's are plotted using the thicker lines.

Figure 1

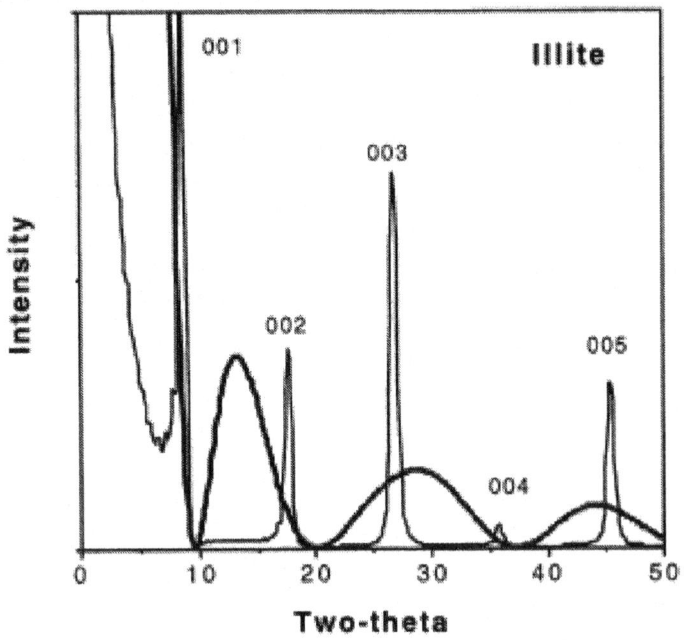

Figure 2

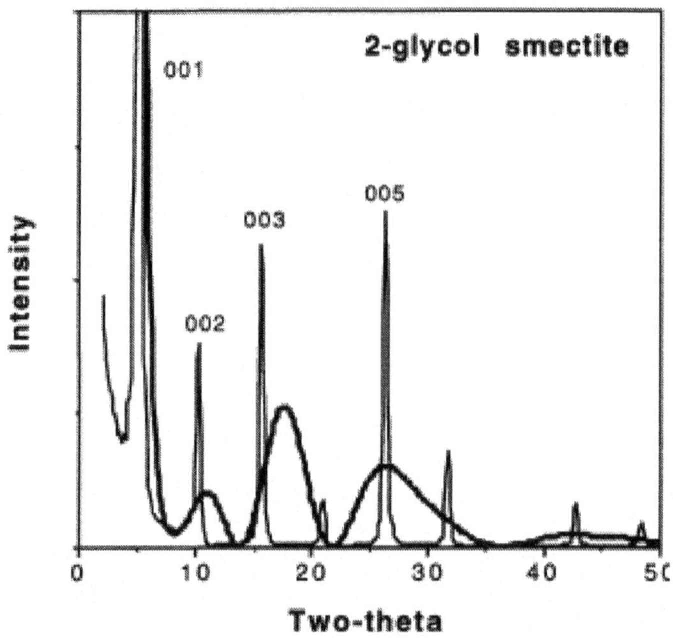

Figure 3

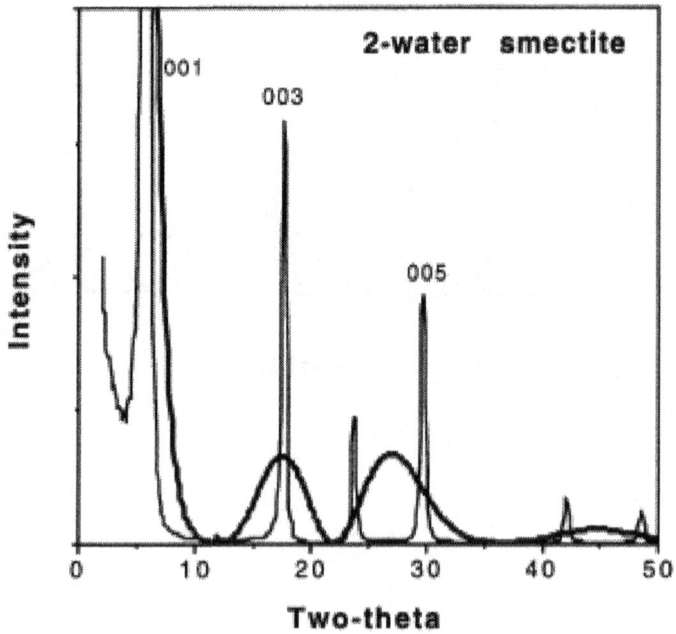

Figure 4

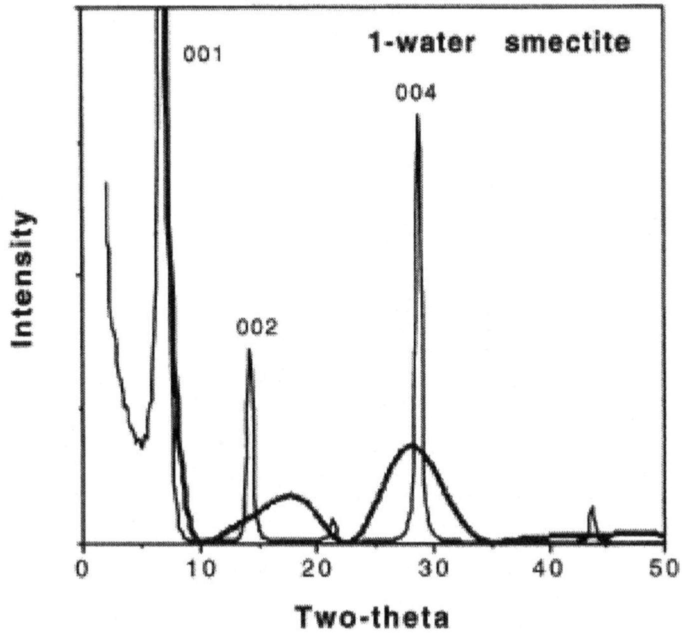

Figure 5

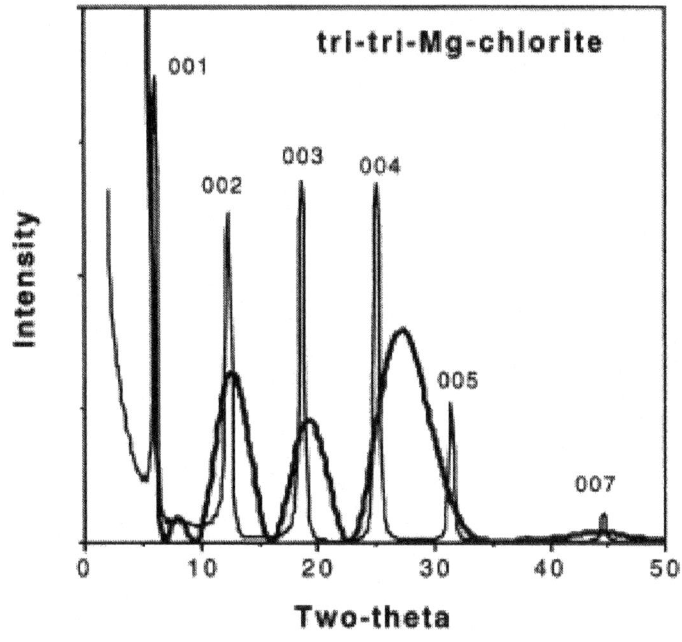

Figure 6

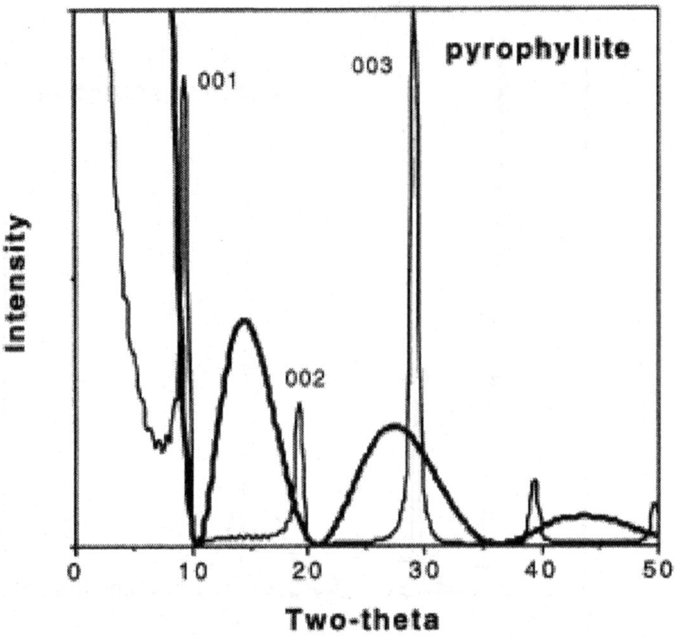

Figure 7

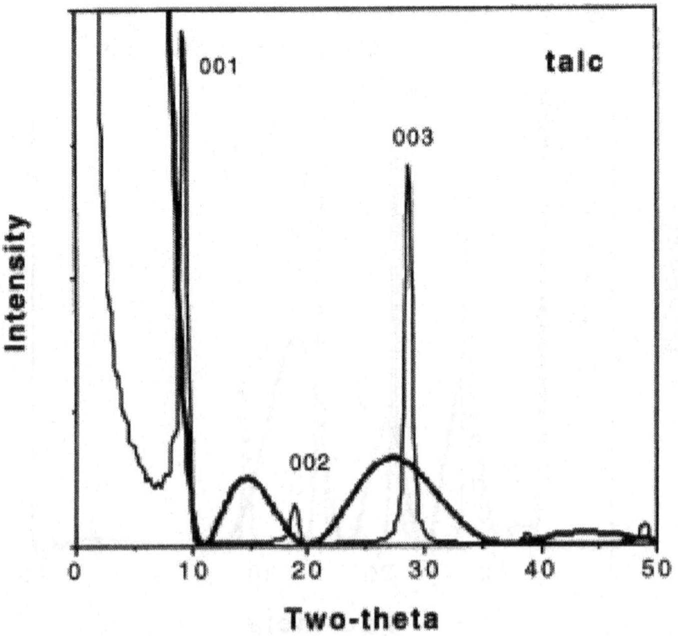

Figure 8

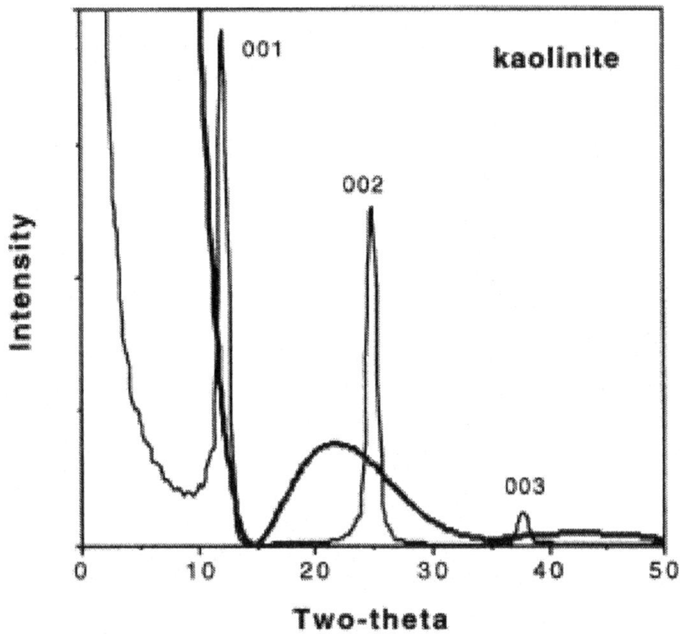

Figure 9

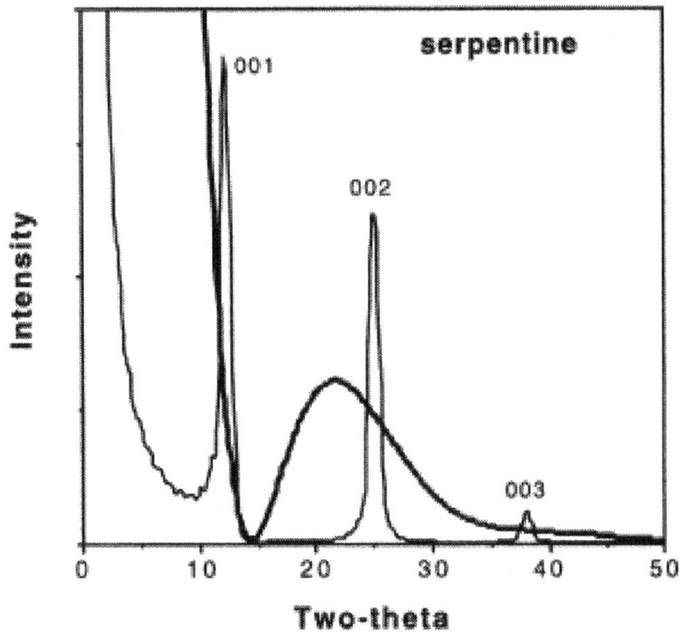

Figure 10

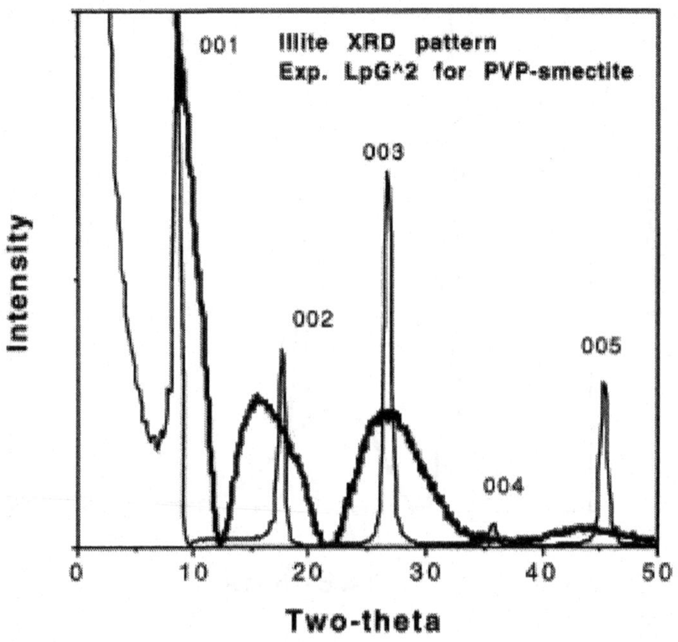
Illite XRD pattern
Exp. LpG^2 for PVP-smectite
001
002
003
004
005
Intensity
Two-theta
0
10
20
30
40
50

APPENDIX 4: ORDER OF CALCULATION AND KEY EQUATIONS

The general order of calculation is as follows:

1. Choose the XRD peak to be studied.
2. Correct intensities for LpG^2.
3. Remove background.
4. Remove K-alpha 2 component of radiation (optional).
5. Flip peak (optional).
6. Perform Fourier analysis of interference function maximum.
7. Remove instrumental broadening from Fourier coefficients (optional).
8. Correct Fourier coefficients for symmetrical (optional) and asymmetrical stain (not installed).
9. Analyze Fourier coefficients for mean crystallite size and crystallite size distribution.
10. Calculate lognormal parameters.
11. Calculate volume distribution.
12. Calculation of illite fixed cations/half-unit cell.
13. Calculation of specific a-b surface area.

The details of the calculations are as follows:

1. Choosing the XRD Peak:

Choose an XRD peak to be analyzed for which the interference function maximum is broadened only by crystallite size and/or stain effects. PeakPicker automatically copies intensities for the peak in two-theta space with respect to the chosen left side of the peak, the peak maximum, and the right side of the peak. These intensities then are pasted into MudMaster. PeakPicker also can choose a peak between any two two-theta angles (asymmetrical option). The maximum intensity from the intensity file is chosen as the peak maximum, so it is important that the top of the peak be smooth. Some commercial programs insure that the XRD peak is smooth by using a mathematical function to model the peak, and this model is used in subsequent analysis. When using this approach it is difficult or impossible to determine crystallite size distributions accurately, because the shape of the XRD peak is determined by the shape of the model. Therefore the approach taken here is to collect good data, and, should it be necessary later in the program (in sheet 2), to smooth the first and second derivatives of the Fourier coefficients when calculating crystallite size distributions (see below). An approximate mean for the peak may be calculated by integral peak width methods (Drits et al., 1997; Eberl et al., 1998), and a line where the background was chosen is plotted on the XRD pattern.

2. Correction of Intensities for LpG^2:

The intensity I(2θ), of an X-ray reflection is calculated as:

$$I(2\theta) = Lp(2\theta)G^2(2\theta)\phi(2\theta) + bg,$$

where Lp is the Lorentz-polarization function, G^2 is the layer scattering intensity (square of the structure factor), ϕ is the interference function, and bg is the background. LpG^2 for several clay minerals have been calculated as a function of two-theta angle in 0.02° steps and are stored in the columns DE:DQ, sheet 1 They were calculated using the program CALCLPG2, which accompanies the MudMaster program. If cell B6, sheet 1, is set to "2," correct LpG^2's for crystal interiors and crystal edges are pasted automatically into columns K and L, respectively, prior to analysis. MudMaster calculates the proportion of crystal edges from the approximate mean thickness, or, if K-saturated, dehydrated illite/smectite is being run, from both the approximate mean thickness and the expandability (see equation 31 in Drits et al., 1998), and weights the sum of the two LpG^2's accordingly. MudMaster then divides LpG^2 into the raw intensities to find the interference function, which contains the crystallite size and strain information of interest.

3. Removal of Background:

If the peak will not be flipped, the smallest intensity values on the left and right sides of the peak are chosen to calculate a curve having an exponential shape that defines the background for the peak. If the peak is to be flipped, then a constant background is chosen from the minimum intensity on the left or right side of the peak, depending on whether the peak will be flipped from left to right or from right to left, respectively. The original intensities at each two-theta angle are corrected for this background curve by subtraction. All intensities to the left and right sides of the left and right background minimums are set equal to zero.

5. Removal of K-alpha 2 Component of the Radiation (optional):

The Fourier method of Gangulee (1970) is used to remove the $K_{\alpha 2}$ component of the radiation. This method requires that the $K_{\alpha 1}$- $K_{\alpha 2}$ angular separation be known, that the $K_{\alpha 1}$ and $K_{\alpha 2}$ components have approximately the same shape, and that the ratio R be known, where R = the maximum intensity of $K_{\alpha 2}$ divided by the maximum intensity of $K_{\alpha 1}$. Gangulee also gives a method for calculating R, because R may differ from the theoretical value of 0.5, depending on the experimental setup. Gangulee's method for calculating R was used in an earlier version of the program, but R always was found to equal 0.5, and therefore the method was removed from MudMaster. However, the readers may want to try this method with their experimental setup to insure that R is 0.5.

$K_{\alpha 2}$ removal is programmed as follows:

(a) The number of data points (N) are found:

$$N = (2\theta_2 - 2\theta_1)/s,$$

where s = the two-theta step size, and $2\theta_1$ and $2\theta_2$ = the beginning and ending two-theta for the theoretical interference function maximum, chosen to begin and end halfway between adjacent orders.

(b) The period for the Fourier series is calculated by transforming the two-theta axis into an axis that is labeled with respect to x, where x ranges from [-(N/2) + 1] to [(N/2) + 1], with the maximum for the interference function intensity located at x = 0.

(c) Delta (Δ), which is the number of two-theta steps between the $K_{\alpha 1}$ and $K_{\alpha 2}$ components, is calculated from:

$$\Delta = \frac{1}{s}\left[2\arcsin\left(\lambda_{\alpha 2}/2d_{(00\ell)}\right) - 2\arcsin\left(\lambda_{\alpha 1}/2d_{(00\ell)}\right)\right],$$

where s = the two-theta step size, $1/d_{(00\ell)}$ is the position in Å^{-1} of the interference function 00ℓ maximum.

(d) The interference function maximum intensity distribution is normalized against the sum of the intensities:

$$I(x)_{norm} = I(x)/\sum I(x).$$

(e) A Fourier analysis of the normalized interference function is carried out according to:

$$A'' = \sum_{-N/2}^{N/2} I(x)_{norm} \cos(2\pi nx/N), \text{ and}$$

$$B'' = \sum_{-N/2}^{N/2} I(x)_{norm} \sin(2\pi nx/N),$$

where "n" is the harmonic number, which equals N/2.

(f) Then p(n) and q(n) are calculated according to:

$$p(n) = 1 + R\cos(2\pi n\Delta/N), \text{ and}$$

$$q(n) = R\sin(2\pi n\Delta/N),$$

where R=0.5.

(g) Then the Fourier coefficients for the $K_{\alpha 1}$ peak are calculated:

$$A'(n) = \left[A''(n)p(n) + B''(n)q(n)\right] / \left[p(n)^2 + q(n)^2\right], \text{ and}$$

$$B'(n) = \left[-A''(n)q(n) + B''(n)p(n)\right] / \left[p(n)^2 + q(n)^2\right]$$

(h) The Fourier coefficients for the $K_{\alpha 1}$ peak are used to construct a new intensity distribution for the interference function with $K_{\alpha 2}$ radiation removed:

$$I_{\alpha 1}(x) = \sum_{n=-\infty}^{\infty} A'(n)\cos 2\pi nx/N + \sum_{n=-\infty}^{\infty} B'(n)\sin 2\pi nx/N.$$

(i) The background then is removed in a manner similar to that described above, except that a linear trend is fitted to the minimum intensity values on the left and right sides of the peak.

5. Flipping the Peak:

If the structure factor approaches zero in the vicinity of an XRD peak, then dividing the intensities by LpG^2 may produce an extremely large intensity for the interference function that is related to the position of the minimum in the layer scattering intensity, rather than to the peak maximum. To avoid this difficulty, one can choose to analyze only half of the XRD peak, and the other half is generated by rotating the analyzed half peak 180° around an axis that passes through the peak maximum.

6. Fourier Analysis of the Interference Function:

A Fourier analysis is performed on either the K_α or the $K_{\alpha 1}$ interference function intensities. This is accomplished as follows:

(a) The previously calculated intensities, I(2θ), for the interference function are normalized to the sum of the intensities:

$$I(2\theta)_{norm} = I(2\theta)/\sum I(2\theta).$$

.(b) The two-theta abscissa is converted into s*, where:

$$s^* = 0.5\left(\frac{s^*_{2\theta} - s^*_{2\theta\,max}}{\Delta s^*}\right), \text{ and}$$

$$s^*_{2\theta} = \frac{2\sin\theta}{\lambda},$$

where the variable θ for the latter equation begins and ends halfway between previous and subsequent reflection orders of the peak, with the maximum of the interference function chosen at s* = 0. $s^*_{2\theta max}$ is calculated in a similar fashion to the latter equation at the two-theta value for the maximum of the interference function, and $\Delta s^* = s^*_{2\theta max} - s^*_{2\theta min}$, where $s^*_{2\theta min}$ is calculated at the minimum two-theta value for the start of the interference function peak.

(c) The maximum n (n_{max}) for the Fourier analysis is calculated from the input (J) in cell A13:

$$n_{max} = (J/d) + 1,$$

where d is the spacing in nm of the peak maximum. The program is limited to a maximum n of approximately 200/d.

(d) A Fourier analysis is performed in which:

$$A(n) = \sum_{s^*=-1/2}^{1/2} I(s^*)_{norm} \cos 2\pi n s^*, \text{ and}$$

$$B(n) = \sum_{s^*=-1/2}^{1/2} I(s^*)_{norm} \sin 2\pi n s^*,$$

where Fourier coefficients are calculated for values of n that increase from zero in increments set in cell A11, sheet 1.

7. Removal of Instrumental Broadening (optional):

Instrumental broadening is removed from the Fourier coefficients by use of the Stokes equation, found in Klug and Alexander (1974):

$$A(n)_{cor} = \left[A(n)_{std} A(n)_{samp} + B(n)_{std} B(n)_{samp}\right] \Big/ \left[A(n)^2_{std} + B(n)^2_{std}\right], \text{ and}$$

$$B(n)_{cor} = \left[B(n)_{samp} A(n)_{std} - A(n)_{samp} B(n)_{std}\right] \Big/ \left[A(n)^2_{std} + B(n)^2_{std}\right],$$

where cor, samp and std refer to the Stokes corrected values, the sample and the standard, respectively. Coefficients for the standard need to have been entered into the program previously, as is discussed in the "Standards" section of this document. It has been found for illite that this correction need not be made if the main thickness is less than approximately 30 nm.

9. Correction of Fourier Coefficients for Strain (optional):

The Fourier coefficients (which, for strain analysis, can be corrected for instrumental broadening by setting cell E7 on sheet 1 to “1”), $A(n)_{cor}$ and $B(n)_{cor}$, now are corrected for strain broadening, if the strain option was chosen, as follows:

(a) $\ln[A(n)_{cor}]$ is calculated for the peak under investigation. These values are stored, according to the analysis number entered into the input in sheet 1, in separate columns for each peak. The square of the reflection order, ℓ^2, also is calculated and stored.

(b) Best-fit straight lines that relate $\ln[A(n)_{cor}]$ values to the abscissa values, ℓ^2, are calculated for each n. Their intercepts on the Y-axis yield the strain corrected Fourier coefficients, $A(n)_{cor}^{D}$, and the slopes of the lines yield the mean strain, $\langle \delta_n^2 \rangle$, for each n. On the assumption that n (or crystallite size) is small:

$$\langle \delta_n^2 \rangle = \left[\ln A(n)_{cor} - \ln A(n)_{cor}^{D}\right] d_{(001)}^2 \Big/ \left[2\pi^2 \ell^2 (n/\ell)\right].$$

The root mean square of the strain (also known as the strain standard deviation) is the square root of this value. It is plotted in Å units as a function of crystallite size for small values of crystallite size in a chart labeled, "Strain Standard Deviation," in sheet 2. The crystallite thickness values over which the root mean square strain is averaged can be changed in cells L11 to L12 in sheet 2. If its value is constant with changing crystallite thickness, then the strain distribution is Gaussian, and the positive half of the strain distribution is presented on a chart labeled, "Strain Distribution." If the root mean square strain is not constant with crystallite thickness, then the Strain Distribution chart has no meaning.

(c) Asymmetrical strain $\langle AS_n \rangle$ was calculated in an earlier version of MudMaster, but was later removed because it did not appear to be useful, especially using flipped peaks. It was calculated as follows:

$$\langle AS_n \rangle = \frac{\arcsin\left(B(n)_{cor} / A(n)_{cor}^{D}\right)}{2\pi\ell}.$$

It can be plotted for $d_{(001)}\langle AS_n \rangle / \sqrt{S}$ as a function of crystallite size (S, in Å units).

9. Calculation of Mean Crystallite Size and Size Distribution:

Mean crystallite size and size distributions are calculated as follows:

(a) The Fourier coefficients determined previously, either corrected $[A(n)^D_{cor}$ or $A(n)_{cor}]$ or not corrected [A(n)] for strain and instrumental broadening, all hereafter referred to simply as H(n), are used to calculate the mean n (here termed $\overline{M}$), and the distribution. The first and second derivative of H(n) are taken with respect to n:

$$\left.\frac{\partial H(n)}{\partial n}\right|_{n\to 0} = \frac{1}{\overline{M}}, \text{ and } \left.\frac{\partial^2 H(n)}{\partial n^2}\right|_{n\to 0} = \frac{f(M)}{\overline{M}}.$$

(b) The hook correction is made by plotting H(n) on the y-axis versus n. The straight line between adjacent points that has the steepest (most negative) slope is extrapolated to n = 0, where H(n) is set equal to one. Extrapolation of this same line in the opposite direction to H(n) = 0 yields the mean crystallite size in terms of n. Mean n is converted into mean size ($\overline{S}$) by the equation: $\overline{S} = \overline{M}d_{(00\ell)}\ell$. The crystallite size distribution is determined by calculating the second derivative of a plot of H(n), not corrected for the hook effect, versus n. N is then converted into size This approach for making the hook correction and for determining the mean crystallite size and the crystallite size distribution was found to be the best method by far, based on trial and error analysis of NEWMOD calculated XRD patterns.

(d) The first and then the second derivative of the plot of H(n) versus crystallite size are smoothed by using a moving average centered on the value to be smoothed. The amount of smoothing is entered in the "Smooth power" option in sheet 2. Both the first and the second derivatives are smoothed. A value of "0" entered here yields no smoothing; a "1" leads to a moving average of 3 centered on the value to be smoothed; a "2" yields a moving average of 5 (two on either side of the value and the value itself), etc. Ends of the data columns are smoothed as much as possible, given the entered smoothing power.

(e) The distribution is truncated by entry of a distribution limit in sheet 2. Truncation eliminates noise in the size and strain distributions at large sizes.

(f) The crystallite size distribution is normalized to the sum of the frequencies, and plotted in a chart on sheet 2.

(g) A mean crystallite size is calculated from the distribution:

$$\bar{S} = \sum f(S)S,$$

where f(S) is the frequency of a given size.

10. Calculation of Lognormal Parameters:

Many natural distributions of crystallite sizes can be approximated by lognormal distributions (Eberl et al., 1990, 1998). A lognormal distribution can be completely described by two parameters, α and β^2:

$$\alpha = \sum f(S)\ln(S),$$

where f(S) is the frequency of a given size, as was calculated in the previous section, and S is the crystallite size; and

$$\beta^2 = \sum f(S)[\ln(S) - \alpha]^2.$$

Then the lognormal size distribution is calculated:

$$g(S) = \left[\frac{1}{S\beta(2\pi)^{0.5}}\right]\exp\left\{-\left(\frac{1}{2\beta^2}\right)[\ln(S) - \alpha]^2\right\}.$$

This theoretical distribution is superimposed as a solid line on the measured crystallite size distribution in sheet 2.

11. Calculation of Volume:

The volume weighted mean size, $\overline{S_v}$, is calculated according to:

$$\overline{S_v} = \frac{\overline{S^2}}{\bar{S}}.$$

12. Calculation of Illite Fixed Cations/Half-Unit Cell:

The fixed cation content of fundamental illite particles per half-unit cell (F_{fix}) is calculated from the particle thiickness (T) and volume-weighted frequencies of those thicknesses [f_v(T)] according to:

$$F_{fix} = \sum \frac{0.89}{T}(T - 1)f_v(T).$$

13. Calculation of Specific a-b Surface Area:

The specific surface area (SSA) of the exposed a-b planes in the crystals is calculated from the density (d, located in cell L16, sheet 2), the particle thicknesses (T) and the volume-weighted frequencies of those thicknesses [f_v(T)] by:

$$SSA = \sum \frac{2000}{dT} f_v(T).$$

APPENDIX 5: HOW TO GET THE LATEST VERSION OF MUDMASTER BY FTP

Push return after each of these steps:

1. Log into your server

2. Type "ftp://brrcrftp.cr.usgs.gov" . Do not type the quotation marks.

3. For the requested name, type "anonymous" .

4. For the password, type your e-mail address.

5. To find the PC version of Mudmaster and associated materials, type:

"cd /pub/ddeberl/pc_version". To find the MAC version, type: "cd /pub/ddeberl/mac_version".

There is a space between cd and /pub...

6. Type "ls" to see the exact file names (the first character of "ls" is lower case L).

7. Type "bin" .

8. Type "get MUDMASTER.EXE" or what ever file you choose to copy after the get command.

The file name is case sensitive.

One also can access the programs from the Internet using the following address:

ftp://brrcrftp.cr.usgs.gov/pub/ddeberl/mac_version/ (or .../pc_version/).

The programs come in self-extracting, compressed versions. Retrieve the Mac versions using Mac Binary; otherwise a Stuffit expander may have to be used. Simply double click on the compressed versions to decompress them. Do not change the file names!

Lightning Source UK Ltd.
Milton Keynes UK
UKOW07f0649250717
305996UK00007B/357/P

9 781287 001294